Eileen Leemputte-Smith, a spiritual writer and advocate for change against social injustice, brings awareness to children of the need to stand up for themselves and others. Untruths and the failure to do the right thing are prevalent in our society and we must teach our children to be champions of both from a very early age. The impact of injustice can have a traumatic effect on how we view the world and ourselves. Eileen's primary focus is to educate school age children to defend themselves against bullying and find commonality among us versus focusing on our differences.

ALWAYS DO your Best

Eileen Leemputte-Smith

AUSTIN MACAULEY PUBLISHERS™

LONDON • CAMBRIDGE • NEW YORK • SHARJAH

Ordering Information

Quantity sales: Special discounts are available on quantity purchases by corporations, associations, and others. For details, contact the publisher at the address below.

Publisher's Cataloging-in-Publication data

Leemputte-Smith, Eileen

Always Do Your Best

ISBN 9781685621018 (Paperback)
ISBN 9781685621025 (ePub e-book)

Library of Congress Control Number: 2024905197

https://www.austinmacauley.com/us

First Published 2024
Austin Macauley Publishers LLC
40 Wall Street, 33rd Floor, Suite 3302
New York, NY 10005
USA

mailto:mail-usa@austinmacauley.com
+1 (646) 5125767

For my children, Liz, Shay, and Joe, whom I love and am so very proud.

I would like to thank my brother, Pete, my defender and champion, whose unending support allowed myself and my children opportunities that would not have been possible without him.

v

My mother once told me
To always do my best
Anything could happen
She said this not in jest

I listened to her say this
Paying less attention than I should
But I knew enough within me
That my best, I always would

The day it came and found me
A surprise my mother was right
I was faced with a decision
Should I do this, I just might

I was sitting in the library
Watching my P's and Q's
When in the distance, I saw them
Of this, I was not amused

A boy of six or seven
Sat hunched upon his chair
Some larger, older classmates
Standing above him, I declare

I jumped up from my station
My P's and Q's be damned
I would not stand the injustice
To this boy who stood no chance

Right over to this victim
Of hap and circumstance
I pushed my way right through them
And took a forward stance

The boys they seemed I'd taken
Them all but by surprise
That a girl of six or seven
Would congregate by *their* side

I grabbed the chair beside me
And stood up upon the seat
To raise my smaller body
Their eyes, I wanted to meet

Now don't think for one darn minute
I'll stand for this, I said
My voice was raised just slightly
My hands above my head

I do not wish to harm you
Your feelings could be hurt
With what I have to tell you
Each of you I will convert

From a bully to a defender
Of those that need your help
Versus being the contender
You must observe yourself

Look at your behavior
To a child just half your size
You've crushed his golden spirit
You can see it in his eyes

You may not see the damage
You've inflicted on this soul
Until you put yourself instead
In a situation beyond your own control

They stood and stared intently
Impressed with my request
And seemed to think a bit differently
Their chins approaching their chests

Tell it to the principal
I'll take you there myself
They'll no doubt call your parents
For it's there you will be dealt

Their shame, it was upon them
It played across their faces
They cleared their throats and shuffled
Their feet were moving places

One boy spoke up quite slowly
A soft and gentle voice
He apologized profusely
Of this he had a choice

My arms, they lowered slightly
My chest, it's beating less
I could hear my mother's voice
The tone she did possess

Her words returned quite quickly
To always do my best
I must have paid attention
This was my first true test

The End